wok

by Vicki Liley

TUTTLE PUBLISHING
Tokyo • Rutland, Vermont • Singapore

Published by Tuttle Publishing, an imprint of Periplus
Editions, with editorial offices at 130 Joo Seng Road,
#06-01, Singapore 368357, and 364 Innovation Drive,
North Clarendon, VT 05759, USA.

Hardcover ISBN 13: 978-0-8048-3920-4
            ISBN 10: 0-8048-3920-4
Printed in Malaysia

Distributed by
North America, Latin America and Europe
Tuttle Publishing, 364 Innovation Drive,
North Clarendon, VT 05759-9436.
Tel: (802) 773-8930 Fax: (802) 773-6993
Email: info@tuttlepublishing.com
www.tuttlepublishing.com

Asia Pacific
Berkeley Books Pte Ltd.
130 Joo Seng Road #06-01
Singapore 368357.
Tel: (65) 6280-1330 Fax: (65) 6280-6290
Email: inquiries@periplus.com.sg
www.periplus.com

10 09 08 07
5 4 3 2 1

TUTTLE PUBLISHING® is a registered trademark of Tuttle Publishing,
a division of Periplus Editions (HK) Ltd.

Contents

All About the Wok

The word wok simply means "cooking vessel" in Cantonese—an indication of how versatile and indeed, indispensable this piece of equipment is for Asian cooks. Its shape, which has remained unchanged for centuries, was originally dictated by the Chinese stove. The stove had an opening in the top into which the round-bottomed wok securely fit.

A wok is a wonderful and practical addition to the contemporary kitchen. The shape accommodates small or large quantities of ingredients and allows control over how they are cooked. The large cooking surface evenly and efficiently conducts and holds heat, making a wok especially well suited for stir-frying, the quick cooking technique used frequently in many Asian cuisines. Although the wok is usually associated with stir-frying, there are few cooking methods for which it cannot be used and a very small number of ingredients that cannot be cooked in it, whether in recipes that are Asian or Western in style.

Of the many woks available, all are basically bowl-shaped with gently sloping sides. Some have looped handles on both sides; others have a long wooden handle on one side. Woks were traditionally made from cast iron and therefore were quite heavy. They are now available in many different materials and finishes. Carbon or rolled steel is one of the best materials. Nonstick woks are easy to clean but may not promote browning of foods as thoroughly as those made of rolled or carbon steel. Other options include stainless steel woks and electric woks, which may not reach temperatures as high as those of cast iron or carbon steel. Round-bottomed woks work best on gas stoves. A stand may be necessary to provide stability; the best choice is a stand with large perforations that promote good heat circulation. Flat-bottomed woks are suited for electric stove tops because they sit directly and securely on the heating element.

Types of Woks

Woks are available in a variety of sizes and materials. A wok with a diameter of 14 in (35 cm) is a versatile size appropriate for the recipes in this book and for other dishes that yield four to six servings. A number of utensils go hand in hand with wok cooking—a lid, a bamboo steamer, a spatula and a slotted spoon.

Cast iron wok

Nonstick woks

Electric wok

Stainless steel wok

Carbon steel wok

Cooking in a Wok

Stir-frying: This technique uses little oil and retains the fresh flavor, color and texture of ingredients. Meat, poultry, seafood, noodles and vegetables are cooked quickly; stirring them constantly helps ensure uniform doneness. The success of stir-frying depends on having all the ingredients ready before cooking starts.

Deep-frying: The wok is ideal for deep-frying as it uses less oil than a deep-fryer and can accommodate ingredients without crowding. Make sure the wok is secure on its stand or heating element before adding the oil. Pour the oil into the wok and heat to 375 °F (190 °C) on a deep-frying thermometer or until a cube of bread sizzles and turns golden brown when dropped into the hot oil.

Stir-frying

Steaming: This method cooks foods with moist heat supplied by boiling water. A bamboo steamer set over, but not touching, the simmering water in a wok is ideal for cooking buns, dumplings, fish, vegetables and puddings. Half-fill a wok with water and bring to a boil. Place the steamer with the food to be cooked over the boiling water and steam covered for the required tim. Lift the steamer off the wok and carefully remove the food from the steamer.

Boiling: A wok can serve as a saucepan, a skillet and a stewing pot, suitable for simmering or reducing a sauce or soup, and boiling vegetables.

Braising: Meat or seafood can be browned to seal in the juices. Once the liquid is added, the wok can be covered for slow simmering.

Deep-frying

Steaming

Boiling

Braising

Cleaning and Seasoning a Wok

Inexpensive carbon-steel or rolled-steel woks sold in Asian stores are coated with a thin film of lacquer to prevent rusting. This film must be removed before a wok can be used. Place the wok on the stove top, fill it with cold water and add 2 tablespoons of baking soda (bicarbonate of soda), then bring the water to a boil and continue boiling rapidly for 15 minutes. Drain and scrub off the coating with a nylon pad. Repeat the process if any coating remains. Rinse and dry the wok and it is now ready to be seasoned.

Carbon steel, rolled steel and cast iron woks require seasoning before food is cooked in them. This process creates a smooth surface that keeps food from sticking to the wok and prevents the wok from discoloring. To season a wok, heat it over low heat. When the wok is hot, carefully wipe it with an oiled paper towel. Continue wiping with fresh towels until they come away clean, without any trace of color. A seasoned wok should not be scrubbed clean with detergent after cooking. Instead, use hot water and a sponge or nylon pad to wipe away any food particles without removing the seasoning layer. Dry the wok well after washing and store it in a dry, well-ventilated place. Long periods without use can cause the oil coating on the wok to become rancid in which case it has to be seasoned again. Using a wok frequently is the best way to prevent this from occurring.

Essential Ingredients

Bean sprouts are most commonly sprouted from green mung beans. They are sold fresh or canned. Fresh sprouts have a crisp texture and a delicate flavor. Store in refrigerator for up to 3 days.

Bok choy is an Asian variety of cabbage with thick white stalks and mild-flavored dark green leaves. Sizes vary from longer than celery stalks to baby bok choy, which are only about 6 in (15 cm) long. If unavailable, use Chinese broccoli or choy sum.

Chili oil is a spicy oil produced by steeping dried red chili peppers in oil. It is available bottled and in jars. Use this hot oil a drop at a time. Store in the refrigerator after opening.

Chinese barbecued pork is made from boneless strips of pork loin that have been marinated in Chinese five spice powder, soy sauce and sugar, and then roasted. It is sold freshly-cooked in slices or strips in Chinese markets. Store up to 2 days in the refrigerator.

Chinese broccoli is a bitter-tasting broccoli with white flowers. Also known as kailan. Regular broccoli and choy sum can be used as a substitute.

Chinese roast duck is sold freshly-roasted in Chinese restaurants and is delicious in stir-fries or on its own. Use 1–2 days after purchase. Substitute barbecued chicken if unavailable.

Choy sum (flowering cabbage) is a popular leafy green vegetable with yellow flowers and thin stalks. Every part of this mild-flavored vegetable can be used. If it is not available, substitute bok choy or Chinese (Napa) cabbage.

Coconut milk is a rich liquid pressed from grated fresh coconut that has been steeped in water. It is used in Asian sauces, curries, soups and desserts. Coconut milk is available canned and in packets.

Coriander leaves, also known as Chinese parsley or cilantro, are the pungent, fragrant leaves of the coriander plant. They have a fresh aroma and flavor and are used widely in Asian cuisines as a herb and as a garnish. Italian parsley or basil may be substituted, although the flavor is not exactly the same.

Curry paste is a condiment

consisting of curry seasonings and red or green chili peppers. Both the Thai red curry paste and green curry paste used in the recipes in this book can be bought ready-made in bottles in most well-stocked supermarkets. Store in the refrigerator after opening.

Dried shrimp paste is produced by drying, salting and grinding shrimp into a pungent-flavored paste that is then formed into blocks or cakes. Known as *belacan* in Malaysia, *kapi* in Thailand, *trasi* in Indonesia and *mam ruoc* in Vietnam, dried shrimp paste is readily available in blocks or plastic containers in Asian food stores. It should be dry-roasted before using.

Fish sauce is a salty, pungent seasoning made from fermented fish. It is sold bottled and varies in intensity depending on the country of origin. Fish

sauce from Thailand, called *nam pla*, is a commonly-available variety.

Garam masala is a hot to mild mixture of ground spices used widely in Indian cooking. The combination, which varies depending on the region of origin and the intended use, usually includes cinnamon, black pepper, coriander, cumin, cardamom, cloves and nutmeg. Pre-blended garam masala can be bought from any Indian spice store or health food store.

Glass noodles, also known as cellophane or bean thread noodles, are thin translucent noodles made from mung bean flour. They are sold in dried form in bundles, and must be soaked in water to soften before using. Rice vermicelli may be used as a substitute.

Hoisin sauce is a sweet, thick Chinese sauce made from soybeans which also contains vinegar, sugar, chili peppers and other seasonings. Bottled

hoisin can be stored indefinitely in the refrigerator. Also known as Chinese barbecue sauce.

Hot bean paste is a spicy hot, thick, red-brown sauce made from fermented soybeans, chili peppers, garlic and spices. Sometimes called red bean paste or chili bean paste, it is available bottled in most large supermarkets.

Kaffir lime leaves are from the kaffir lime tree and are used to add an enticing citrusy flavor and aroma to soups, curries and other dishes. Grated lime rind may be used as a substitute.

Lemongrass is a tropical grass whose pale stalks lend

| Shiitake mushrooms | Oyster mushroom | Dried black Chinese mushrooms | Straw mushrooms |

The **mushrooms** used in this book include **shiitake mushrooms**, **straw mushrooms** and **oyster mushrooms**. These are all available fresh, or in dried or canned form from Asian markets. **Dried black Chinese mushrooms** have a stronger flavor than fresh shiitake mushrooms, although two may be used interchangeably. Soak dried mushrooms in hot water for 30 minutes or until soft, then discard the tough stem before using.

an intense lemony flavor to curries, soups, stir-fries and other dishes. The thick lower part of the stem nearest the bottom is the edible portion. Trim off the green top part and peel away the dry outer leaves of the thick lower stem. Bruise or slice the inner core for cooking, Lemongrass is available fresh in most supermarkets.

Mirin is a sweet alcoholic wine made from rice and used in Japanese cooking. Sweet sherry can be substituted.

Miso is a thick paste of fermented ground soybeans, used in Japanese soups and other dishes. It is available in various color and flavors. Light-colored varieties of miso are milder in flavor than dark-colored pastes. Red and white misos are the most common and they can be found in Asian markets. Chinese bean paste or fermented bean sauce may be used as a substitute.

Oyster sauce is a thick, dark brown sauce made from dried oysters and soy sauce,

and used to impart an intense or mild briny flavor to stir-fries and other dishes. Store in the refrigerator after opening. Soy sauce may be used as a substitute.

Palm sugar is a type of sugar made from the juice of palm fruits. It varies in color from gold to dark brow and has a rich flavor similar to dark brown sugar, molasses or maple syrup, all of which make good substitutes. Available in Asian markets in packets and plastic containers. Shave with a sharp knife or grate before using.

Rice vinegar is a mild vinegar produced from fermented rice. Japanese and Chinese rice vinegars can be found in Asian stores and well-stocked supermarkets.

Rice wine is a low-alcohol wine, also known as Shaoxing wine or Shaoxing yellow rice wine. It is brewed from fermented glutinous rice. Sake or dry sherry can be substituted.

Sambal oelek is an Indonesian spice paste consisting of ground chili peppers combined with salt, sugar and vinegar. Other sweet chili pastes may be used as a substitute.

Sesame oil is a strong-tasting golden-colored oil pressed from roasted sesame seeds, used mainly as a flavoring.

Spring roll wrappers are thin sheets of rice flour, used to enclose savory fillings. Sometimes called spring roll skins, they are sold frozen in the supermarket. They should be defrosted and separated before using and kept, covered with a damp kitchen towel to prevent them from drying out while you are preparing the fillings.

Thai sweet chili sauce is used as a flavoring and as a dipping sauce. It is sold bottled in most supermarkets. Store in the refrigerator after opening. To make your own: Bring $1/2$ cup (125 ml) of water and $1/2$ cup (125 ml) of rice vinegar to a boil, and stir in $1/2$ cup (100 g) of sugar, 2 teaspoons each of minced fresh ginger, garlic, chili pepper, fish sauce and tomato ketchup. Simmer over low heat for 5 minutes and thicken with 1 tablespoon of cornstarch before removing from the heat.

Tofu is made from soybeans that have been dried, soaked, cooked and pressed to form cakes that range in texture from soft to firm. **Silken** or **soft tofu** has a very fine texture, high water content and tends to break easily. **Firm tofu** holds its shape better when cut or cooked and has a slightly sour taste. **Pressed tofu** is firm tofu with much of the moisture extracted and is therefore firmer and is excellent for stir-fries. Tofu is available in the refrigerated sections of most supermarkets in packets, blocks and cylinders.

Water chestnuts are the root of a plant grown in Asia, round in shape with a sweet, and crunchy flesh. Water chestnuts are widely available canned. After opening, store them in clean water in the refrigerator for up to 3 weeks. Fresh water chestnuts can be purchased in Asian markets and must be peeled before using. If unavailable, use diced celery for a texture substitute.

Wonton wrappers are thin sheets of wheat dough, square or circular in shape, used to enclose a variety of fillings. Available fresh or frozen. Also called wonton skins or dumpling wrappers.

Shrimp Dumplings

16–18 wonton wrappers

1 egg, lightly beaten, for brushing

Green onion (scallion) strips, to garnish

Soy sauce, for dipping

Filling

8 oz (250 g) fresh shrimp, peeled and deveined

3 fresh or canned water chestnuts, finely chopped

2 green onions (scallions), minced

2 teaspoons soy sauce

$1/_2$ teaspoon sesame oil

Makes 16–18 dumplings

1 Prepare the Filling by processing the shrimp in a food processor until smooth, or mincing them well. Transfer to a bowl, add all the other ingredients and mix until well combined.

2 To make the dumplings, place a wonton wrapper on a work surface and spoon 1 tablespoon of the Filling to the center. Brush the edges of the wrapper with the beaten egg, then lift and gather the edges together and twist to seal, forming a nice little pouch. Continue to make the dumplings in the same manner with the remaining ingredients.

3 Line a bamboo steamer with parchment (baking) paper and arrange the dumplings on top. Half-fill a wok with water and bring to a rapid boil. Cover the bamboo steamer and place it over the boiling water. Steam the dumplings for 20 minutes until cooked.

4 Arrange the dumplings on individual serving platters and garnish with green onion strips. Serve warm with a dipping bowl of soy sauce on the side.

Mini Spring Rolls with Sweet Chili Dip

Twenty-five 4-in (10-cm) square
  spring roll or wonton wrappers
2 teaspoons cornstarch mixed
  with 2 tablespoons water, for
  brushing
Oil, for deep-frying

Crabmeat Filling
2 teaspoons oil
1 cup (100 g) thinly-sliced baby
  bok choy leaves and stems
3 kaffir lime leaves, finely sliced
  into thin shreds, or 1 teaspoon
  grated lime rind
1 cup (4 oz/125 g) cooked crabmeat
2 tablespoons chopped coriander
  leaves (cilantro)
2 teaspoons soy sauce
2 teaspoons freshly-squeezed
  lime juice

Dipping Sauce
1 tablespoon fish sauce
3 tablespoons freshly-squeezed
  lime juice
1 green onion (scallion), minced
1 small red finger-length chili pepper, deseeded and chopped
1 tablespoon shaved palm sugar
  or dark brown sugar
1 tablespoon finely-chopped
  coriander leaves (cilantro)
1 tablespoon rice wine vinegar
$1/2$ small cucumber, peeled,
  deseeded and finely chopped

1 Prepare the Crabmeat Filling first by heating the oil in a wok and stir-frying the bok choy over high heat until softened, about 1 minute. Remove from the heat and allow to cool. Add all the other ingredients and mix well. Set aside.

2 To make the spring rolls, place a wrapper on a work surface and spoon 1 heaped tablespoon of the Crabmeat Filling to the center. Fold the wrapper in half diagonally, enclosing the filling. Tuck in both sides and roll up tightly into a cylinder. Half-way reaching the top corner, brush the edges of the wrapper with the cornstarch mixture, then continue rolling until the end, pressing to seal. Repeat to make the spring rolls with the remaining ingredients.

3 Heat the oil in a wok to 375 °F (190 °C)—the oil is ready when a small bread cube dropped in it sizzles and turns golden. Working in batches, carefully lower the spring rolls into the hot oil and deep-fry, turning often, until crispy and golden on all sides, 1–2 minutes. Using a slotted spoon, remove the spring rolls from the hot oil and drain on paper towels.

4 Combine the Dipping Sauce ingredients in a bowl and mix well.

5 Serve the spring rolls immediately with a bowl of Dipping Sauce on the side.

Makes about 25 mini spring rolls

Steamed Vegetable Buns

Dough

1 teaspoon active dry yeast

$1/_2$ cup (125 ml) warm water

4 tablespoons superfine (castor)
  sugar

1 cup (125 g) all-purpose flour

$1/_2$ cup (60 g) self-rising flour

1 tablespoon melted butter

Filling

3 dried black Chinese mushrooms

2 teaspoons sesame oil

2 cloves garlic, minced

1 teaspoon grated fresh ginger

$1/_2$ small leek, chopped

1 cake pressed tofu (5 oz/150 g),
  chopped

$1/_2$ small carrot, peeled and grated

1 tablespoon chopped roasted
  cashew nuts

2 teaspoons freshly-squeezed
  lime juice

2 teaspoons Thai sweet chili sauce

1 teaspoon hot bean paste

1 tablespoon tomato paste

Makes 16 buns

1 Make the Dough first by combining the yeast, 2 tablespoons of the warm water, 1 teaspoon of the sugar and 1 teaspoon of the flour in a small bowl and mixing well. Cover and allow to ferment in a warm place until frothy, about 15 minutes.

2 Sift the remaining flour and self-rising flour into a mixing bowl. Add the yeast mixture and the remaining warm water and sugar, and mix with a wooden spoon until the mixture forms a soft Dough. On a floured work surface, knead the Dough by hands until it is smooth and elastic, 3–5 minutes. Cover and allow the Dough to rise in a warm place until it doubles in volume.

3 To prepare the Filling, soak the dried mushrooms in hot water until softened, 15–30 minutes. Drain and squeeze out the liquid. Remove and discard the thick stems from the mushrooms and thinly slice the caps.

4 Heat the sesame oil in a wok and stir-fry the garlic, ginger and leek over medium heat until fragrant and soft, about 1 minute. Add the tofu, carrot and chopped cashew nut and stir-fry for 2–3 minutes until heated through, seasoning with the lime juice, chili sauce, bean and tomato pastes. Remove from the heat and set aside to cool.

5 Punch down the Dough and turn it out onto the floured work surface. Knead the Dough by hands for about 5 minutes, then divide it into 16 equal pieces. Roll or press each piece to form a $2^1/_2$-in (6-cm) circle. Cover the circles with a damp cloth to prevent them from drying out. Working with a circle at a time, spoon 1 tablespoon of the Filling to the center of the circle, then gather the edges together and twist to seal into a bun. Set aside, covered with the cloth. Continue to make the buns in the same manner with the remaining ingredients.

6 Cut out 16 squares of parchment (baking) paper and place the buns, sealed side down, on the paper. Half-fill a wok with water and bring to a rapid boil. Working in batches, arrange the buns in a steamer, cover and place the steamer over the boiling water. Steam the buns for 15–20 minutes until cooked. Serve warm.

Crispy Shrimp Toasts

24 slices white bread
2 tablespoons sesame seeds
Oil, for deep-frying
Bottled sweet chili sauce,
   for dipping

Shrimp Paste
4 Asian shallots, peeled
2 cloves garlic, peeled
1 small red finger-length chili
   pepper, deseeded
1 stalk lemongrass, thick bottom
   part only, dry outer layers
   discarded, inner part sliced
10 oz (300 g) fresh shrimp,
   peeled and deveined
1 egg white
1 tablespoon fish sauce
2 teaspoons freshly-squeezed
   lemon juice
3 kaffir lime leaves, cut into thin
   shreds, or 1 teaspoon grated
   lime rind
2 tablespoons minced coriander
   leaves (cilantro)

1 Prepare the Shrimp Paste first by processing the shallots, garlic, chili and lemongrass in a blender or food processor until smooth. Add the shrimp and continue to process to a smooth paste. Transfer to a large bowl, add all the other ingredients and mix well. Set aside.

2 Using a 3-in (8-cm) star- or round-shaped cookie cutter, cut out a star or round shape from each slice of bread (reserve the leftover bread for other use). Spread 1 heaped tablespoon of the Shrimp Paste on the center of each star- or round-shaped bread, pressing down gently so it sticks on, then sprinkle with the sesame seeds.

3 Heat the oil in a wok to 375 °F (190 °C)—the oil is ready when a small bread cube dropped in it sizzles and turns golden. Working in batches, carefully lower the coated bread into the hot oil and deep-fry until crispy and golden on both sides, 1–2 minutes. Using the slotted spoon, remove the shrimp toasts from the heat and drain on paper towels. Serve hot with a dipping bowl of sweet chili sauce on the side.

Makes 24 toasts

Crispy Chicken or Pork Wontons

40 wonton wrappers
1 egg, lightly beaten
Oil, for deep-frying

Filling
1 tablespoon oil
1 small onion, chopped
1 clove garlic, minced
1 cup (7 oz/200 g) ground chicken
  or pork
1 tablespoon chunky peanut butter
2 teaspoons Thai sweet chili sauce
2 teaspoons fresh lemon juice
2 tablespoons chopped coriander
  leaves (cilantro)

Makes about 20 fried wontons

1 To prepare the Filling, heat the oil in a wok and stir-fry the onion and garlic over medium heat until fragrant and soft, about 1 minute. Add the ground meat and stir-fry for 1 minute. Remove from the heat and stir in all the other ingredients. Allow the Filling to cool completely.
2 To make the wontons, place a wrapper on a work surface and spoon 1 tablespoon of the Filling to the center. Brush the edges of the wrapper with the beaten egg, then place another wrapper on top and firmly press the edges together to seal. Repeat to make the wontons in the same way with the remaining ingredients.
3 Heat the oil in a wok to 375 °F (190 °C)—the oil is ready when a small bread cube dropped in it sizzles and turns golden. Working in batches, carefully lower the wontons into the hot oil and deep-fry, turning often, until crispy and golden on both sides, 1–2 minutes. Remove from the hot oil and drain on paper towels. Serve hot with chili oil if desired.

Spiced Chicken Wings

1 tablespoon ground turmeric
2 teaspoons ground red pepper
1 tablespoon ground coriander
1 tablespoon ground cumin
3 cloves garlic, minced
12 chicken wings
Oil, for deep-frying
Lime wedges, to serve
Bottled sweet chili sauce,
  for dipping

Makes 12 deep-fried wings

1 Combine the spices in a small bowl and mix well, then rub into each chicken wing with your fingers until well coated. Place the coated wings in a dish, cover and refrigerate for 2 hours.
2 Heat the oil in a wok to 375 °F (190 °C)—the oil is ready when a small bread cube dropped in it sizzles and turns golden. Deep-fry the chicken wings, a few at a time and turning often, until golden and crisp, 3–4 minutes. Using a slotted spoon, remove from the hot oil and drain on paper towels. Keep the cooked wings warm while deep-frying the remaining wings.
3 Serve the chicken wings with lime wedges and a dipping bowl of sweet chili sauce.

Crispy Wontons with Roast Duck Filling

20 green onions (scallions), white part only, cut into 3-in (8-cm) lengths

2 carrots, peeled and cut into 3-in (8-cm) sticks

Oil, for deep-frying

20 square wonton wrappers

1 Chinese roast duck, meat and skin separated and coarsely chopped

$1/2$ cup (125 ml) hoisin sauce, to serve

Makes 20

1 Using a sharp knife or scissors, make several shallow cuts into both ends of each green onion length to make fringes. Soak the green onion and carrot in a bowl of iced water until the green onion curls, about 15 minutes.

2 Heat the oil in a wok to 375 °F (190 °C)—the oil is ready when a small bread cube dropped in it sizzles and turns golden. Working with a wonton wrapper at a time and using two sets of tongs, hold the wrapper in taco shape and lower it into the hot oil. Continue to hold the wrapper until it is golden and crisp, 30 seconds–1 minute. Lift the deep-fried wrapper from the hot oil and drain on paper towels. Repeat to deep-fry the remaining wonton wrappers.

3 To serve, fill each fried wrapper with a green onion length, several carrot sticks and some duck meat. Arrange on a serving platter, drizzle with hoisin sauce and serve immediately.

Steamed Rice and Pork Meatballs

1 cup (200 g) uncooked rice
Soy sauce, for dipping

Meatballs
2 cups (14 oz/400 g) ground pork
3 green onions (scallions), chopped
3 fresh or canned water chestnuts,
  chopped
1 tablespoon oyster sauce
2 tablespoons minced coriander
  leaves (cilantro)
2 cloves garlic, minced
1 tablespoon grated fresh ginger
1 tablespoon soy sauce
1 tablespoon Thai sweet chili sauce

1 Wash the rice and soak it in water for 30 minutes, then drain and spread out on a tray lined with paper towels to dry.
2 Combine the Meatballs ingredients in a bowl and mix well. Wet your hands, spoon 1 heaped tablespoon of the mixture and shape it into a ball, then roll the Meatball in the rice until well coated on all sides. Continue to make the rice coated Meatballs in the same manner with the remaining ingredients.
3 Half-fill a wok with water and bring the water to a rapid boil. Arrange the Meatballs in a steamer, allowing space for the rice to expand. Cover and place the steamer over the boiling water in the wok and steam for 20 minutes until cooked. Serve the Meatballs hot with dipping bowls of soy sauce on the side.

Makes 32 or serves 4–6

Spicy Stir-fried Pork Appetizers

1 tablespoon oil
2 cloves garlic, minced
1 tablespoon grated fresh ginger
3 green onions (scallions), chopped
$1/2$ teaspoon dry shrimp paste
1 tablespoon chopped lemongrass
1–2 teaspoons sambal oelek or
  other bottled chili pastes
7 oz (200 g) ground pork
10 cherry tomatoes, quartered
1 tablespoon thick coconut milk
1 teaspoon salt, or to taste
2 tablespoons chopped coriander
  leaves (cilantro)
Belgian endive or butter lettuce
  leaves, to serve

1 Heat the oil in a wok and stir-fry the garlic, ginger, green onion, shrimp paste, lemongrass and sambal over medium heat until fragrant, 1–2 minutes. Add the pork and toss well until it changes color, 1–2 minutes.
2 Stir in the tomatoes and coconut milk and cook until the tomatoes soften slightly, 1–2 minutes. Season with the salt and remove from the heat, then add the coriander leaves and mix well.
3 Spoon the pork filling onto the endive or lettuce leaves and serve hot.

Serves 4

Fish Cakes with Sweet Chili Sauce

$1/_2$ cup (125 ml) oil, for frying
Thai sweet chili sauce, for dipping

Fish Cakes
10 oz (300 g) fresh white fish fillets
  or ground fish
2 teaspoons fish sauce
2 teaspoons oyster sauce
1–2 teaspoons sambal oelek or
  other bottled chili pastes
1 egg white, lightly beaten
2 cloves garlic, minced
2 tablespoons cornstarch
4 kaffir lime leaves, cut into thin
  shreds
4 tablespoons chopped green
  onions (scallions)

1 To make the Fish Cakes, process the fish fillets to a smooth paste in a blender or food processor. Omit this step if using ground fish. Transfer to a bowl, add all the other ingredients and mix until well blended. Wet your hands, spoon 2 tablespoons of the mixture and roll it into a ball, then flatten it slightly with the palm to form a patty. Continue to shape the patties in the same manner with the remaining ingredients.
2 Heat the oil in a wok over medium heat until hot and fry the patties, a few at a time, until golden and cooked, 1–2 minutes on each side. Remove from the heat and drain on paper towels. Serve hot with dipping bowls of Thai sweet chili sauce on the side.

Makes 12 fish cakes

Crispy Shrimp and Pork Wontons

Thirty-two 3-in (8-cm) square
  wonton wrappers
Oil, for deep-frying
Bottled sweet chili sauce or plum
  sauce, to serve

Filling
8 oz (250 g) fresh shrimp, peeled
  and deveined
1 cup (7 oz/200 g) ground pork
3 fresh or canned water chestnuts,
  finely chopped
1 tablespoon minced coriander
  leaves (cilantro)
2 teaspoons cornstarch
1 egg, lightly beaten
$1/_2$ teaspoon sesame oil
2 teaspoons fish sauce
$1/_2$ teaspoon salt
$1/_4$ teaspoon ground white pepper

1 Prepare the Filling first by processing the shrimp to a smooth paste in a blender or food processor, or mincing them well. Transfer to a large bowl, add the ground pork, water chestnut, minced coriander leaves, cornstarch and $1/_2$ of the beaten egg and mix well. Stir in all the seasonings and mix until well blended.

2 To make the dumplings, place a wonton wrapper on a work surface and spoon 1 tablespoon of the Filling to the center. Brush the edges of the wrapper with the remaining beaten egg, then lift and gather the edges of the wrapper together and twist to seal, forming a nice little pouch. Continue to make the dumplings in the same manner with the remaining ingredients.

3 Heat the oil in a wok to 375 °F (190 °C)—the oil is ready when a small bread cube dropped in it sizzles and turns golden. Working in batches, deep-fry the dumplings, turning often, until crispy and golden on all sides, 1–2 minutes. Remove from the hot oil and drain on paper towels. Serve hot with dipping bowls of sweet chili sauce or plum sauce.

Makes 32 fried dumplings

Chicken Broth with Crabmeat Dumplings

6 cups (1$^1/_2$ liters) chicken stock

3 slices fresh ginger

2 stalks lemongrass, thick bottom part only, dry outer layers discarded, inner part chopped

1 teaspoon salt, or to taste

$^1/_2$ teaspoon ground white pepper, or to taste

1 green onion (scallion), cut into strips, to garnish

Crabmeat Dumplings

$^1/_2$ cup (60 g) cooked crabmeat or $^1/_2$ cup (100 g) ground shrimp

$^1/_2$ cup (100 g) ground pork

2 teaspoons grated fresh ginger

1 tablespoon chopped coriander leaves (cilantro)

1 egg, beaten

2 teaspoons soy sauce

2 teaspoons oyster sauce

$^1/_2$ teaspoon ground white pepper

Few drops sesame oil

1 Prepare the Crabmeat Dumplings by combining all the ingredients in a large bowl and mixing well. Wet your hands, spoon 1 tablespoon of the mixture and roll it into a ball. Continue making the Crabmeat Dumplings until all the mixture is used up. Set aside.

2 Bring the chicken stock and spices to a boil in a wok. Reduce the heat to low and simmer, uncovered, for about 5 minutes. Remove from the heat and strain. Discard the spices and return the broth to the wok.

3 Bring the broth to a boil again over medium heat. Add the Crabmeat Dumplings and simmer uncovered for 2–3 minutes until firmed and cooked. Season with the salt and pepper and remove from the heat.

4 Spoon the Crabmeat Dumplings into individual serving bowls and ladle the hot broth over. Garnish with the green onion strips and serve immediately.

Serves 4

Clear Chicken Soup with Chinese Mushroom

6 dried black Chinese mushrooms
6 cups (1$^1/_2$ liters) chicken stock
2 cloves garlic, minced
1 teaspoon grated fresh ginger
2 teaspoons rice vinegar
2 teaspoons shaved palm sugar or
  dark brown sugar
7 oz (200 g) boneless chicken
  breasts, sliced
2 green onions (scallions), sliced
1 stalk lemongrass, thick bottom
  part only, dry outer layers
  discarded, inner part sliced
1 red finger-length chili pepper,
  deseeded and chopped
1 teaspoon salt, or to taste
$^1/_2$ teaspoon ground white
  pepper, or to taste

1 In a bowl, soak the mushrooms in hot water until softened, 15–30 minutes. Drain and squeeze out the liquid from the mushrooms. Remove and discard the thick stems and thinly slice the caps. Set aside.
2 Bring the chicken stock, garlic, ginger, vinegar and sugar to a boil in a wok over high heat. Reduce the heat to low and simmer, uncovered, for about 5 minutes.
3 Stir in the sliced mushrooms and all the other ingredients, increase the heat and return to a boil. Reduce the heat to low again, cover and simmer for 5–10 minutes until the chicken is cooked. Taste and adjust the seasonings, then remove from the heat. Ladle into individual serving bowls and serve hot.

Serves 4

Vegetable Soup with Coconut

1 tablespoon oil
1 clove garlic, minced
4 tablespoons chopped coriander
  (cilantro) stems
4 green onions (scallions), chopped
$1/4$ teaspoon dried shrimp paste
5 cups ($1^1/_4$ liters) chicken stock
1 cup (250 ml) thick coconut milk
2 teaspoons sambal oelek or other
  bottled chili pastes
$1/_2$ head green cabbbage (7 oz/
  200 g), cut into thin shreds
12 snowpeas, trimmed and sliced
1 carrot, peeled and cut into strips
1 cup (100 g) broccoli florets
2 tablespoons freshly-squeezed
  lime juice, or to taste
1 tablespoon fish sauce, or to taste

1 Heat the oil in a wok and stir-fry the garlic, coriander, green onion and shrimp paste over medium heat until fragrant, 1–2 minutes.
2 Add the chicken stock, coconut milk and sambal and bring to a boil. Reduce the heat to a simmer, add the vegetables and cook uncovered until tender, about 5 minutes. Season with the lime juice and fish sauce, adjusting the seasoning as desired. Remove from the heat, ladle into individual serving bowls and serve hot.

Serves 4

Miso Soup with Scallops

8 oz (250 g) fresh shucked scallops, sliced in half

4 in (10 cm) fresh ginger, peeled, thinly sliced into shreds

4 tablespoons chopped coriander leaves (cilantro)

1$^1/_2$ cups (375 ml) water

1 stalk lemongrass, thick bottom part only, dry outer layers discarded, inner part finely chopped

4 kaffir lime leaves, finely sliced into thin shreds, or 1 teaspoon grated lime rind

2 tablespoons miso paste

1 teaspoon freshly-squeezed lime juice

1 Bring the scallop halves, ginger, coriander leaves, water, lemongrass and lime leaf shreds or grated rind to a boil in a wok over high heat. Reduce the heat and simmer covered until the scallop changes color, 1–2 minutes. Remove from the heat and strain, reserving the broth. Keep the cooked scallop and spices warm.

2 Return the broth to the wok and top up with some water to make 4 cups (1 liter). Bring to a boil over high heat, then stir in the miso paste and lime juice. Reduce the heat and simmer covered for about 3 minutes. Taste and adjust the seasonings as desired, then remove from the heat. Ladle the hot Miso soup into individual serving bowls and serve alongside the scallop.

Serves 4

Creamy Carrot Soup with Coconut and Chili

1 tablespoon oil
1 teaspoon sesame oil
1 small red finger-length chili pepper, deseeded and chopped
4 cloves garlic, minced
1 tablespoon grated fresh ginger
2 onions, peeled and chopped
2 lbs (1 kg) carrots, peeled and sliced
1 teaspoon ground cumin
1 teaspoon ground turmeric
4 cups (1 liter) thick coconut milk
2 cups (500 ml) chicken stock
Salt and ground white pepper, to taste
Tarragon leaves, to garnish

1 Heat the oils in a wok and stir-fry the chili, garlic and ginger over medium heat until fragrant, about 1 minute. Add the chopped onion, carrot, cumin and turmeric and stir-fry for 2–3 minutes.
2 Pour in the coconut milk and chicken stock and bring to a boil. Reduce the heat to low and simmer uncovered until the carrot has softened, about 15 minutes. Remove from the heat and set aside to cool, then process to a purée in a blender or food processor.
3 Return the purée to the wok and heat through for about 2 minutes, stirring. Taste and season with the salt and pepper, then remove from the heat. Ladle into individual serving bowls and serve warm, garnished with the tarragon leaves.

Serves 4–6

Noodles with Salmon in Spicy Coconut Broth

7 oz (200 g) dried glass (bean thread) or rice noodles
1 tablespoon oil
1 teaspoon sesame oil
4 cups (1 liter) thick coconut milk
3 cups (750 ml) fish stock
8 oz (250 g) fresh salmon fillets, thinly sliced
2 tablespoons freshly-squeezed lemon juice
1 tablespoon fish sauce, or to taste
2 green onions (scallions), sliced
4 tablespoons mint leaves

Spice Paste
3 small red finger-length chili peppers, deseeded
3 cloves garlic, peeled
2 in (5 cm) fresh ginger, peeled and sliced
1/2 cup (20 g) coriander leaves (cilantro)

1 Soak the glass noodles in water until soft, 5–10 minutes, then drain and set aside. If using dried rice noodles, half-fill a saucepan with water and bring to a boil, then cook the noodles for 3–5 minutes until soft.
2 Process the Spice Paste ingredients in a blender or food processor until smooth.
3 Heat the oils in a wok and stir-fry the Spice Paste over medium heat until fragrant, 1–2 minutes. Stir in the coconut milk and fish stock, and bring to a boil. Reduce the heat to low and simmer uncovered for about 10 minutes.
4 Add the salmon slices and season with the lemon juice and fish sauce, then cook for 2–3 minutes until the fish is opaque. Add the glass or rice noodles and continue to simmer for 1 more minute. Taste and adjust the seasoning as desired and remove from the heat. Divide the noodles equally among serving bowls and ladle the hot soup over. Sprinkle with the green onion and mint leaves and serve hot.

Serves 6

Classic Shrimp and Pork Fried Rice

1 tablespoon grated fresh ginger

1 teaspoon ground turmeric

1 teaspoon dried shrimp paste

2 teaspoons bottled chili sauce

3 tablespoons oil

1 onion, chopped

3 cloves garlic, minced

$1/2$ red bell pepper, deseeded and chopped

1 stalk celery, chopped

1 carrot, peeled and chopped

$1/2$ cup (75 g) fresh or frozen peas

1 cup (50 g) bean sprouts, trimmed

1 cup (100 g) thinly-sliced green cabbage or bok choy leaves and stems

4 cups (400 g) cold cooked rice, grains separated

$1/4$ lb (125 g) fresh shrimp, peeled, tails intact

$1/4$ lb (125 g) Chinese barbecued pork, diced

$1/4$ cup (60 ml) coconut milk

2 tablespoons soy sauce

1 Combine the ginger, turmeric, shrimp paste and chili sauce in a small bowl and mix well. Set aside.

2 Heat the oil in a wok and stir-fry the onion over medium heat for about 1 minute, then add the garlic and stir-fry until lightly browned. Add all the vegetables and stir in the ginger mixture. Increase the heat to high and stir-fry until the vegetables are tender, 2–3 minutes.

3 Add the rice, shrimp and barbecued pork, and toss until heated through, 1–2 minutes. Stir in the coconut milk and soy sauce and stir-fry until well blended. Remove from the heat, spoon the fried rice into individual serving bowls and serve hot as the main course or as an accompaniment to other stir-fried dishes.

Serves 6

Thai Fried Rice

3 tablespoons oil

1 onion, chopped

1 red finger-length chili pepper, deseeded and chopped

1 tablespoon Thai red curry paste (page 14)

5 oz (150 g) boneless pork loin, thinly sliced

12 oz (350 g) fresh large shrimp (about 12), peeled and deveined, tails intact

4 cups (400 g) cold cooked rice, grains separated

2 eggs, beaten

$1/2$ cup (30 g) chopped green onions (scallions)

$1/3$ cup (15 g) chopped coriander leaves (cilantro)

1 tablespoon fish sauce, or to taste

3 red finger-length chili peppers, cut into "flowers" (see note), to garnish

1 Heat the oil in a wok and stir-fry the onion and chili over medium heat until fragrant and soft, 1–2 minutes. Stir in the red curry paste and cook for 1 minute. Add the pork slices and stir-fry for 1–2 minutes until well coated with the curry paste, then stir in the shrimp and toss until the shrimp turn pink.

2 Add the rice and toss well to combine, 1–2 minutes. Make a well in the center and add the beaten egg. Cook the egg until partially set, then mix well with the rice. Stir in the green onion and coriander leaves and season with the fish sauce. Stir-fry for 1 more minute until the rice is heated through. Remove from the heat. Garnish with red chili flowers if desired and serve hot as the main course or as an accompaniment to stir-fried dishes.

Note: To make the red chili "flowers", using a sharp knife, make several closely spaced cuts into $2/3$ the length of a red finger-length chili pepper, then soak the chili in iced water until it curls, about 15 minutes.

Serves 4–6

Ginger Rice with Herbs and Coconut

2 tablespoons oil
1 teaspoon chili oil
1 onion, chopped
3 cloves garlic, minced
1 tablespoon grated fresh ginger
1 red bell pepper, deseeded and chopped
$1^1/_2$ cups (300 g) uncooked short-grain rice
$1^1/_2$ cups (375 ml) chicken stock
$^1/_2$ cup (125 ml) thick coconut milk
1 cup (250 ml) water
1 teaspoon salt, or to taste
3 green onions (scallions)
3 tablespoons chopped coriander leaves (cilantro)
6 tablespoons dried unsweetened grated (desiccated)
   coconut
2 tablespoons freshly-squeezed lemon juice, or to taste
Chinese barbecued pork slices, to serve

1 Heat both oils in a wok and stir-fry the onion, garlic and ginger over medium heat until fragrant and soft, 1–2 minutes. Add the bell pepper and stir-fry for 1 more minute, then stir in the rice and toss until well blended.
2 Add the chicken stock, coconut milk, water and salt, and bring to a boil. Reduce the heat to low, cover and simmer until all the liquid has been absorbed and the rice is cooked, 15–20 minutes. Remove from the heat and stir in the green onion, coriander leaves, $^1/_2$ of the grated coconut and lemon juice. Transfer to individual serving platters, top with the remaining grated coconut and serve hot with the barbecued pork slices alongside.

Serves 4–6

Classic Roast Pork Chao Mian

1 lb (500 g) fresh egg noodles, or 8 oz (250 g) dried
  egg noodles or thin spaghetti
1 tablespoon oil
2 teaspoons sesame oil
3 cloves garlic, minced
2 cups (200 g) sliced Chinese broccoli or cabbage
1 cup (50 g) bean sprouts, trimmed
8 oz (250 g) Chinese barbecued pork, sliced

Seasonings
$1/_2$ cup (125 ml) peanut butter
2 tablespoons soy sauce
1–2 teaspoons sambal oelek, or other bottled chili paste

1 Bring a saucepan of water to a boil and blanch the
fresh noodles for 30 seconds–1 minute. If using dried
egg noodles, blanch for several more minutes until soft.
Remove from the heat, drain and set aside.
2 Heat the oils in a wok and stir-fry the garlic over
medium heat until fragrant, about 30 seconds. Add the
vegetables and sir-fry for 1–2 minutes, then stir in the
noodles and pork slices. Add the Seasonings ingredients
and toss well to combine, about 1 minute. Do not
overcook. Remove from the heat, transfer to serving
platters and serve hot.

Serves 4

Classic Chicken Chao Mian

Oil, for deep-frying
1 lb (500 g) fresh thin egg noodles
  or angel hair pasta
3 cloves garlic, minced
1 in (3 cm) fresh ginger, peeled
  and grated
1 onion, cut into eighths
2 chicken thigh fillets, skins
  removed, cubed
1 red and 1 green bell pepper,
  deseeded and sliced
1$^1/_2$ cups (150 g) sliced choy sum,
  bok choy or cabbage
3 tablespoons hoisin sauce
$^1/_4$ cup (60 ml) chicken stock,
  mixed with 1 tablespoon cornstarch

1 Heat the oil in a wok until hot and deep-fry the egg noodles over medium heat until golden and crisp, 1-2 minutes. Using a slotted spoon, remove from the hot oil and drain on paper towels. Distribute the noodles equally among serving platters and set aside.
2 Heat 2 tablespoons of the oil in a clean wok and stir-fry the garlic, ginger and onion over medium heat until fragrant and soft, about 1 minute. Stir in the chicken meat and toss until it changes color, then add the vegetables and stir-fry for about 2 minutes until tender and cooked. Stir in the hoisin sauce and chicken stock mixture, and cook until the sauce has thickened. Remove from the heat, ladle over the deep-fried noodles and serve hot

Serves 4

Fettuccine with Baked Vegetables

1 lb (500 g) fresh fettuccine or
  8 oz (250 g) dried fettuccine
2 cups (150 g) butternut squash,
  peeled and cut into bite-sized
  pieces
5 cloves garlic, minced
3 tablespoons oil
1 zucchini, sliced
1 onion, diced
1 cup (250 ml) thick coconut milk
$1/_4$ cup (10 g) chopped coriander
  leaves (cilantro)
1 small finger-length red chili
  pepper, deseeded and chopped
1 teaspoon salt, or to taste
$1/_4$ teaspoon ground white pepper

Serves 4

1 Preheat the oven to 400 °F (200 °C).
2 Bring a saucepan of water to a boil. Add 1 teaspoon of salt and blanch the fresh fettuccine for 1–2 minutes until warmed through. If using dried fettuccine, blanch for 10–12 minutes until soft. Remove from the heat and drain. Set aside.
3 Combine the squash pieces, $1/_2$ of the minced garlic and 2 tablespoons of the oil in a baking dish and toss until the vegetable is coated well with the oil, then bake, uncovered, for 15 minutes. Remove from the oven, add the zucchini pieces and mix well, then return to the oven and bake for 15 more minutes until the vegetables are tender.
4 Heat the remaining oil in a wok and stir-fry the onion and remaining garlic over medium heat until fragrant and soft, 1–2 minutes. Add the coconut milk, coriander leaves and chopped chili, and simmer uncovered for 2–3 minutes until heated through. Stir in the baked vegetables and noodles and season with the salt and pepper, then remove from the heat. Divide the noodles among individual serving platters and serve immediately.

Stir-fried Noodles with Sliced Peppers and Mushrooms

1 lb (500 g) fresh egg noodles, or
   8 oz (250 g) dried egg noodles
6 dried black Chinese mushrooms
1 tablespoon oil
2 teaspoons sesame oil
1 red and 1 yellow bell pepper,
   deseeded and sliced
1 cup (50 g) bean sprouts, trimmed
7 oz (200 g) fresh oyster mushrooms, sliced
$^1/_4$ cup (60 ml) Thai sweet chili
   sauce
1 tablespoon soy sauce
Coriander leaves (cilantro),
   to garnish

Serves 4

1 Bring a saucepan of water to a boil and blanch the
fresh noodles for 30 seconds–1 minute. If using dried
egg noodles, blanch for 2–3 minutes until soft.
Remove from the heat, drain and set aside.
2 Soak the dried mushrooms in hot water, covered,
for 15-30 minutes until soft. Drain and squeeze out the
soaking liquid. Remove and discard the thick stems from
the mushrooms, then thinly slice the caps. Set aside.
3 Heat the oils in a wok and stir-fry the Chinese mushroom slices over medium heat until fragrant, about 1
minute. Add the vegetables and oyster mushroom,
and stir-fry until tender, 1–2 minutes. Stir in the
sauces, then add the noodles and toss until heated
through and well combined, 1–2 minutes. Do not
overcook. Remove from the heat, transfer to serving
platters and serve hot, garnished with coriander leaves
(cilantro).

Simple Chicken with Vegetable Stir-fry

6 dried black Chinese mushrooms
2 tablespoons oil
3 cloves garlic, minced
1 red finger-length chili pepper, deseeded and finely chopped
3 chicken thigh fillets, skins removed, sliced
6 asparagus spears, cut into short lengths
2 cups (200 g) sliced bok choy, choy sum or cabbage
1 cup (100 g) sugar snap peas or snow peas, trimmed
Crisp deep-fried egg noodles (optional), to serve

Sauce
$1/_4$ cup (60 g) chicken stock
1 tablespoon soy sauce or black bean paste, or to taste
1 tablespoon rice wine
1 teaspoon sesame oil

1 Soak the dried mushrooms in hot water, covered, for 15–30 minutes until soft. Drain and squeeze out the soaking liquid. Remove and discard the thick stems from the mushrooms, then thinly slice the caps. Set aside.

2 Combine the Sauce ingredients in a small bowl and mix well. Set aside.

3 Heat the oil in a wok and stir-fry the garlic and chili over medium heat until fragrant, 1-2 minutes. Add the mushroom and chicken slices and stir-fry until the meat changes color. Stir in all the vegetables and toss for about 2 minutes until tender. Pour in the Sauce and continue tossing for 1 more minute until the ingredients are heated through and well combined. Remove from the heat and serve hot with crisp deep-fried egg noodles if desired.

Serves 4

Thai Green Curry Chicken with Coconut

2 tablespoons oil

2 cloves garlic, minced

1 onion, chopped

1–2 tablespoons Thai green curry paste (page 14)

4 chicken thigh fillets (1 lb/500 g total), skins removed, cut into thin strips

8 oz (250 g) green beans, trimmed and halved

4 kaffir lime leaves, torn, or 1 teaspoon grated lime rind

2 cups (500 ml) thick coconut milk

1 cup (250 ml) water or chicken stock

2 tablespoons chopped coriander leaves (cilantro), (optional)

1 tablespoon fish sauce, or to taste

1 tablespoon freshly-squeezed lime juice

1 tablespoon palm sugar or dark brown sugar

Thai basil leaves, cut into thin shreds, to garnish

1 Heat the oil in a wok and stir-fry the garlic and onion over medium heat until fragrant and tender, 1-2 minutes. Add the green curry paste and stir-fry for 1–2 minutes, then add the chicken, green beans, kaffir lime leaves or lime rind and stir-fry for 2–3 minutes until the chicken has just cooked through.

2 Stir in the coconut milk and water or chicken stock, and bring slowly to a boil. Reduce the heat to low and simmer uncovered for 3–5 minutes until slightly thickened. Stir in the chopped coriander leaves (if using) and season with the fish sauce, lime juice and sugar, adjusting the taste. Cook for 1 more minute, then remove from the heat. Transfer to serving bowls, garnish with the basil leave shreds and serve with steamed rice.

Serves 4–6

Simple Pork and Vegetable Stir-fry

2 tablespoons oil

3 cloves garlic, peeled and minced

1 small red finger-length chili pepper, deseeded and chopped

1 lb (500 g) pork, thinly sliced

2 cups (200 g) sliced choy sum, bok choy or cabbage

3 kaffir lime leaves, finely cut into thin shreds, or 1 teaspoon grated lime rind

1 tablespoon soy sauce

2 teaspoons freshly-squeezed lime juice

2 firm nectarines, pitted and sliced (optional)

Heat the oil in a wok over high heat and stir-fry the garlic and chili until fragrant, about 30 seconds. Add the pork, vegetable and lime leaves and stir-fry until the pork changes color, 1–2 minutes. Season with the soy sauce and lime juice and continue to stir-fry until heated through, 1–2 more minutes. Add the nectarines (if using), mix well and remove from the heat. Serve hot with steamed rice.

Serves 4–6

Roast Duck with Green Beans Stir-fry

2 teaspoons oil
2 green onions (scallions), chopped
1 in (3 cm) fresh ginger, peeled
  and grated
8 oz (250 g) green beans, cut into
  short lengths
1 tablespoon grated orange rind
1 tablespoon mirin
1 tablespoon soy sauce
$1/2$ Chinese roast duck (purchased
  from a Chinese market or restau-
  rant), cut into serving pieces

Heat the oil in a wok and stir-fry the green onion and ginger over medium heat until fragrant and tender, 1–2 minutes. Add the beans and grated orange rind and stir-fry until cooked, 2–3 minutes, then season with the mirin and soy sauce, adjusting the taste. Stir in the roast duck pieces and remove from the heat. Serve hot with steamed rice.

Serves 4

Thai Beef Curry with Mushrooms and Basil

8 oz (250 g) beef sirloin or top round

1 tablespoon oil

2 cloves garlic, minced

1 tablespoon Thai red curry paste (page 14)

1 cup (250 ml) thick coconut milk

2 teaspoons fish sauce

1 tablespoon shaved palm sugar or dark brown sugar

1 cup (80 g) fresh or canned baby corn

$1/3$ cup (70 g) drained canned straw mushrooms

$1/4$ cup (10 g) Thai basil leaves, to garnish

1 Freeze the beef wrapped in plastic wrap in the freezer until slightly firm, about 30 minutes. Remove from the freezer, unwrap and slice thinly.

2 Heat the oil in a wok and stir-fry the garlic and beef slices over high heat for about 1 minute. Remove from the heat and set aside.

3 Heat the red curry paste in the wok over medium heat until it begins to bubble, about 30 seconds. Stir in the coconut milk, fish sauce, sugar, corn and mushrooms, and bring to a boil. Reduce the heat to a simmer and cook for 1–2 minutes. Return the beef to the wok and toss until heated through, then cover and simmer for 1 minute, until the beef is cooked. Taste and adjust the seasoning as desired and remove from the heat. Sprinkle with basil leaves and serve hot with steamed rice.

Serves 4

Beef Curry with Potato

2 tablespoons oil
1 lb (500 g) beef sirloin or top
  round, cubed
1 cup (250 ml) water
2–3 sweet potatoes or potatoes,
  peeled and cut into chunks
1 teaspoon salt, or to taste
1 red and 1 green finger-length
  chili pepper, deseeded and
  sliced

Spice Paste
1 onion, peeled
2 cloves garlic, peeled
1 stalk lemongrass, thick bottom
  part only, dry outer layers
  discarded, inner part sliced
1 teaspoon dried shrimp paste
1 teaspoon ground cumin
2 teaspoons ground coriander
$1/2$ teaspoon ground turmeric
1 teaspoon ground paprika
1 teaspoon grated lime rind
1 teaspoon oil

1 Prepare the Spice Paste first by processing the onion, garlic and lemongrass in a blender or food processor until smooth. Transfer to a bowl, add all the other ingredients and mix well.
2 Heat the oil in a wok and stir-fry the beef over medium heat until browned, 2-3 minutes. Remove from the heat and drain on paper towels.
3 Reheat the wok and stir-fry the Spice Paste over medium heat until fragrant, about 1 minute. Return the beef to the wok, pour in the water and bring the ingredients to a boil. Reduce the heat to low, cover and simmer, stirring occasionally, for about 15 minutes. Stir in the potato chunks and cook for 10 minutes until tender, adding a little more water if necessary. Season with the salt and remove from the heat. Transfer to serving bowls and sprinkle with the chili slices. Serve immediately with steamed rice.

Serves 6

Stir-fried Beef with Chinese Greens

10 oz (300 g) beef sirloin or top
round
4 cloves garlic, minced
1 in (3 cm) fresh ginger, peeled
and grated
3 tablespoons oil
1 red finger-length chili, deseeded
and chopped
1 teaspoon sambal oelek, or other
bottled chili paste
$1^1/_2$ cups (150) sliced choy sum,
bok choy or Chinese cabbage
$1^1/_2$ cups (150 g) sugar snap peas
or snow peas, trimmed
1 cup (50 g) bean sprouts,
trimmed
1 tablespoon oyster sauce
1 teaspoon salt, or to taste

1 Freeze the beef in the freezer wrapped in plastic wrap until slightly firm, about 30 minutes, then thinly slice. In a bowl, combine the beef slices with the garlic, ginger and 1 tablespoon of the oil and mix well. Cover and refrigerate for 30 minutes.

2 Heat a wok and stir-fry the beef slices over medium heat until browned, 1–2 minutes. Remove from the heat and drain on paper towels.

3 Heat the remaining oil in a clean wok and stir-fry the chili and sambal until fragrant, about 1 minute. Add the vegetables and stir-fry until tender-crisp, 1–2 minutes. Return the beef slices to the wok, season with the oyster sauce and salt, and stir-fry until heated through and well combined, 1–2 minutes. Remove from the heat and serve hot with steamed rice.

Serves 4

Chili Lime Shrimp

1 lb (500 g) fresh shrimp, peeled and deveined, tails
  intact
Pinch of ground red pepper
$1/4$ teaspoon ground turmeric
3 tablespoons oil
3 cloves garlic, minced
1 red finger-length chili pepper, deseeded and
  chopped
1 teaspoon black mustard seeds (optional)
1 tablespoon freshly-squeezed lime juice
Lime wedges, to serve

1 Combine the shrimp, red pepper and turmeric in a
large bowl and mix well. Set aside.
2 Heat the oil in a wok and stir-fry the garlic, chili and
mustard seeds (if using) over medium heat until the
seeds begin to pop, 1–2 minutes. Increase the heat to
high, add the spiced shrimp and stir-fry until pink and
cooked, 2–3 minutes. Remove from the heat and stir in
the lime juice. Arrange the shrimp on a serving platter
and serve immediately with the lime wedges.

Serves 4

Ginger Coconut Shrimp

2 tablespoons oil
2 onions, chopped
1 lb (500 g) fresh shrimp, peeled, tails intact
2 ripe tomatoes, diced
$3/4$ cup (175 ml) thick coconut milk
2 teaspoons cracked black peppercorns
2 tablespoons chopped coriander leaves (cilantro)

Spice Paste
2 in (5 cm) fresh ginger, peeled and sliced
4 cloves garlic, peeled
1 in (3 cm) fresh turmeric root, peeled and sliced, or
   1 teaspoon ground turmeric
1 small red finger-length chili pepper, deseeded
2 tablespoons white vinegar

1 Prepare the Spice Paste first by processing all the ingredients in a blender or food processor until smooth. Set aside.
2 Heat the oil in a wok and stir-fry the onion and Spice Paste over medium heat for 2–3 minutes. Add the shrimp and stir-fry until pink, then stir in the chopped tomato and cook until soft, 1– 2 minutes.
3 Pour in the coconut milk, reduce the heat to low and simmer covered for about 5 minutes. Stir in the black pepper and chopped coriander leaves (cilantro), and remove from the heat. Serve immediately with steamed rice.

Serves 4–6

Beer Batter Shrimp with Mango Salsa

1$^1/_2$ cups (185 g) all-purpose flour
1 teaspoon baking powder
1 teaspoon salt
$^1/_2$ teaspoon dried chili flakes
1 teaspoon brown sugar
1 can (12 oz/400 ml) beer
Oil, for deep-frying
2 lbs (1 kg) fresh jumbo shrimp, peeled, tails intact
Lime wedges, to serve

Mango Salsa
1 ripe mango, peeled, pitted and diced
2 green onions (scallions), chopped
$^1/_2$ small red finger-length chili pepper, deseeded and
  chopped
3 tablespoons freshly-squeezed lime juice
2 teaspoons sesame oil
$^1/_2$ cup (20 g) chopped Asian basil
Ground white pepper, to taste

1 Combine the Mango Salsa ingredients in a bowl and mix well. Set aside.
2 Sift the flour and baking powder into a large bowl, then add the salt, chili flakes and sugar. Pour in the beer and using a wooden spoon, mix the mixture into a smooth batter.
3 Heat the oil in a wok to 375 °F (190 °C)—the oil is ready when a bread cube dropped in it sizzles on contact. Working with a few at a time, dip the shrimp into the batter to coat well, then deep-fry in the hot oil until golden brown on all sides, 30–60 seconds. Remove from the heat and drain on paper towels.
4 Arrange the deep-fried shrimp on serving platters and serve hot with the lime wedges and Mango Salsa on the side.

Serves 4

Shrimp and Avocado Salad with Grapefruit Dressing on Crisp Wontons

Oil, for deep-frying
12 wonton wrappers

Grapefruit Dressing
$1/4$ cup (60 ml) freshly-squeezed grapefruit juice
$1/4$ cup (60 ml) olive oil
2 teaspoons shaved palm sugar or dark brown sugar
1 tablespoon white wine vinegar
1 teaspoon grated fresh ginger

Shrimp and Avocado Salad
2 tablespoons oil
3 cloves garlic, minced
1 lb (500 g) fresh shrimp, peeled, tails intact
$1/2$ avocado, peeled, pitted and chopped
1 ripe tomato, diced
$1/2$ onion, diced
$1/4$ cup (10 g) chopped coriander leaves (cilantro)

Serves 4

1 Prepare the Grapefruit Dressing by combining all the ingredients in a screw-top jar and shaking the jar until the ingredients mix well. Set aside.

2 To make the Shrimp and Avocado Salad, heat the oil in a wok and stir-fry the garlic over medium heat until fragrant, 30 seconds–1 minute. Add the shrimp and stir-fry until pink, 2–3 minutes. Remove from the wok and drain on paper towels. Set aside to cool, then combine with the avocado, tomato, onion and coriander leaves (cilantro) in a large bowl. Add the Grapefruit Dressing and toss until well blended. Cover and allow to stand for 10 minutes for the flavors to develop.

3 Heat the oil in a wok to 375 °F (190 °C)—the oil is ready when a bread cube dropped in it sizzles on contact. Working in batches, deep-fry the wonton wrappers until golden and crisp, about 30 seconds on each side. Remove the deep-fried wrappers from the hot oil and drain on paper towels.

4 To serve, place a fried wonton wrapper on each serving platter and pile some Salad on it, then position another fried wonton wrapper on top of the Salad and spoon on the second layer of Salad. Finish off the arrangement by laying the third deep-fried wonton wrapper on top.

Fish with Coconut Rice and Tomato Salsa

1 lb (500 g) white fish fillets
2 teaspoons grated fresh ginger
$1/_4$ teaspoon ground coriander
Pinch of ground turmeric
1 small onion, finely chopped
1 green finger-length chili pepper,
  deseeded and chopped
2 tablespoons dried unsweetened
  grated (desiccated) coconut
1 clove garlic, minced
4 whole cloves
$1^1/_2$ tablespoons freshly-squeezed
  lime juice

Coconut Rice

1 cup (200 g) uncooked glutinous
  rice
1 tablespoon oil
1 onion, chopped
1 teaspoon ground cardamom
$1/_2$ cup (125 ml) water
$1/_2$ cup (125 ml) thick coconut
  milk
Pinch of salt

Tomato Salsa

2 ripe tomatoes, diced
$1/_4$ cup (10 g) chopped coriander
  leaves (cilantro)
3 tablespoons freshly-squeezed
  lime juice
1 kaffir lime leaf, cut into thin
  shreds, or $1/_2$ teaspoon grated
  lime rind

1 Rinse the fish well, then pat dry with paper towels and set aside. Combine the ginger, ground coriander, turmeric, onion, chili pepper, grated coconut, garlic and cloves in a small bowl, pour in enough lime juice and mix the mixture into a thick paste. Spread the spice paste into both sides of each fillet until well coated. Place the coated fillets in a heatproof dish, cover and refrigerate until ready to steam.

2 To make the Coconut Rice, wash the glutinous rice in a couple of changes of water and drain well. Heat the oil in a wok and stir-fry the onion over medium heat until fragrant and soft, about 1 minute. Remove from the heat. Place the stir-fried onion and oil with all the other ingredients in a saucepan and stir well, then cover tightly and bring to a boil over medium heat. Reduce the heat to low and simmer until all the liquid has been absorbed and the rice is cooked, 10–15 minutes. Remove from the heat, allow to stand covered for 10 minutes, then fluff the cooked rice with a fork. Alternatively, place the ingredients in a rice cooker and cook as you would the normal rice.

3 Half-fill a large wok with water and bring to a rapid boil. Place the dish with the fish in a bamboo steamer, cover and stand the steamer over the boiling water in the wok. Steam for 8–10 minutes (depending on the thickness of the fillets) until the fish is cooked.

4 Combine the Tomato Salsa ingredients in a bowl and mix well. Set aside.

5 Spoon the fillets to individual serving platters and top with the Tomato Salsa. Add the Coconut Rice on the side and serve immediately.

Serves 4

Stir-fried Squid or Octopus with Vegetables

1 lb (500 g) squids or baby
  octopus
2 tablespoons oil
1 red finger-length chili pepper,
  deseeded and halved
1$^1/_2$ cups (150 g) sliced green
  beans
4 kaffir lime leaves, finely sliced
  into thin shreds, or 1 teaspoon
  grated lime rind
1$^1/_2$ cups (150 g) snow peas,
  trimmed

Marinade
1 tablespoon soy sauce
1 tablespoon oil
1 tablespoon dry sherry or sake
2 cloves garlic, minced
2 teaspoons grated lime rind
2 tablespoons freshly-squeezed
  lime juice

1 Clean the squids thoroughly, discarding the heads but retaining the tentacles. Remove the cartilage in the center of the tentacles. Halve each tube lengthwise and rinse the inside well. Using a sharp knife, score the flesh by making diagonal criss-cross slits across the surface, then slice into $^3/_4$-in (2-cm) strips. If using baby octopus, rinse them well, removing and discarding the heads and the little hard ball or "beak" in the center of each octopus.
2 Place the squid or octopus in a glass or ceramic bowl. Combine the Marinade ingredients in a small bowl, then pour over the squid or octopus and mix until well coated. Cover and refrigerate for 1 hour.
3 Heat the oil in a wok and stir-fry the chili pepper over high heat until fragrant, about 30 seconds. Add the vegetables and stir-fry until tender-crisp, about 2 minutes. Stir in the squid or baby octopus with the Marinade and stir-fry for 1–2 minutes until just cooked through (do not overcook or the seafood will toughen). Remove from the heat and serve immediately.

Serves 4

Spiced Fried Whole Snapper

4 small snappers (each 8 oz /250 g)
Oil, for deep-frying
2 parsnips (each 5 oz/150 g),
  peeled
Lime wedges, to serve

Spice Paste
2 teaspoons ground cumin
1 green finger-length chili pepper,
  deseeded
$1/_2$ cup (20 g) coriander leaves
  (cilantro)
3 cloves garlic, peeled
1 in (3 cm) fresh ginger, peeled
  and sliced
2 teaspoons garam masala, or
  cajun spice mix

1 Prepare the Spice Paste first by processing all the ingredients in a blender or food processor until smooth. Set aside.

2 Gut and clean the fish, then pat dry with paper towels. Using a sharp knife, make several shallow diagonal cuts into both sides of each fish, then rub the Spice Paste into the fish, coating it well on both sides. Leave the fish to marinate in the refrigerator for 1 hour.

3 Heat the oil in a wok to 375 °F (190 °C)—the oil is ready when a bread cube dropped in it sizzles on contact. Deep-fry the fish, one at a time and turning over once, until golden brown and crisp on both sides, about 4 minutes. Remove from the heat and drain on paper towels. Keep warm.

4 Thinly slice each parsnip lengthwise using a vegetable peeler. Reheat the oil in a clean wok and deep-fry the parsnip slices until golden and crispy, about 1 minute. Remove from the wok and drain on paper towels.

5 Arrange the deep-fried fish and parsnip chips on individual serving platters and serve immediately with the lime wedges.

Serves 4

Scallops with Pesto and Mashed Potatoes

1 lb (500 g) potatoes or sweet potatoes, peeled and cut into chunks
2 tablespoons olive oil
3 cloves garlic, minced
2 tablespoons oil
1 small red finger-length chili pepper, deseeded and chopped
1 lb (500 g) fresh shucked scallops, halved if large
1 tablespoon freshly-squeezed lime juice
Lime wedges, to serve

Pesto

2 cups (60 g) fresh basil leaves
4 tablespoons pine nuts, dry-roasted
4 tablespoons grated parmesan cheese
Ground white pepper, to taste
2 cloves garlic, minced
$1/4$ cup (60 ml) extra-virgin olive oil

1 Prepare the Pesto by processing all the ingredients except the olive oil in a food processor until finely chopped. With the motor running, gradually pour in the olive oil and continue to process until well blended. Set aside.

2 Half-fill a saucepan with water and bring to a boil over high heat. Add the potatoes and simmer over medium heat, uncovered, until tender, about 10 minutes. Remove from the heat and drain. Transfer to a large bowl and mash with a fork or a potato masher. Stir in the olive oil and $2/3$ of the minced garlic. Keep warm until ready to use.

3 Heat the oil in a wok and stir-fry the chili and remaining garlic over medium heat until fragrant, about 1 minute. Add the scallops and stir-fry for 2–3 minutes until just cooked, taking care not to overcook or the scallops will toughen. Remove from the heat and stir in the lime juice.

4 To serve, spoon the mashed potato or sweet potato onto individual serving platter and top with $1/4$ of the Pesto. Arrange the scallops on top of the Pesto and serve hot, accompanied with lime wedges. Store any leftover Pesto in a sealed container in the refrigerator.

Serves 4

Simple Tofu and Vegetable Stir-fry

$1/_3$ cup (100 ml) oil

2 cakes pressed or firm tofu,
10–12 oz (300–400 g), sliced
into cubes

3 cloves garlic, minced

1 in (3 cm) fresh ginger, peeled
and grated

2 onions, sliced

$1^1/_2$ cups (150 g) sliced Chinese
broccoli or bok choy

1 cup (100 g) snow peas, trimmed

1 red bell pepper, deseeded and
sliced

1 cup (80 g) fresh or canned baby
corn (optional)

$1^1/_2$ cups (150 g) sliced spinach or
cabbage

2 tablespoons oyster sauce

1 tablespoon soy sauce

1 Heat the oil in a wok over medium heat until hot. Working in batches, fry the tofu cubes until golden brown on all sides, 2–3 minutes. Remove from the heat and drain on paper towels.

2 In a clean work, heat 2 tablespoons of the oil and stir-fry the garlic, ginger and onion over medium heat until fragrant and lightly browned, 1–2 minutes. Add all the other vegetables and stir-fry for 2–3 minutes until tender.

3 Stir in the fried tofu cubes and season with the oyster and soy sauces. Continue stir-frying for 1 more minute and remove from the heat. Transfer to a serving platter and serve hot with steamed rice.

Serves 4

Spiced Squash and Lentil

4 cups (300 g) butternut squash
  or pumpkin, peeled and cubed
$1/_2$ cup (100 g) dried lentils
1 tablespoon oil
1 red chili pepper, deseeded and
  chopped (optional)
1 teaspoon cumin seeds
2 teaspoons coriander seeds,
  cracked
Sprigs of coriander leaves
  (cilantro), to garnish

Dressing
$1/_3$ cup (100 ml) olive oil
2 teaspoons grated lime rind
$1/_3$ cup (100 ml) freshly-squeezed
  lime juice
2 tablespoons chopped coriander
  leaves (cilantro)
$1/_2$ teaspoon sugar
Ground white pepper, to taste

1 Prepare the Dressing first by combining all the ingredients in a screw-top jar and shaking the jar until the ingredients mix well. Set aside.

2 Half-fill a wok with water and bring to a rapid boil. Place the squash or pumpkin cubes in a heatproof dish and place the dish in a steamer. Cover the steamer and stand it over the boiling water in the wok. Steam the squash or pumpkin cubes until they are tender, 10–12 minutes. Remove from the heat and set aside to cool.

3 Place the lentils in a saucepan with enough water to cover. Bring to a boil over medium heat and cook until tender (but do not overcook), about 5 minutes. Remove from the heat, drain and set aside to cool.

4 Heat the oil in a wok and stir-fry the chili pepper (if using), cumin and coriander seeds over medium heat until fragrant, 1–2 minutes. Add the steamed squash or pumpkin and lentils, and stir-fry until well blended, about 1 minute. Remove from the heat, pour in the Dressing and toss well to combine. Serve warm or chilled, garnished with coriander leaves (cilantro).

Serves 4

Sugar Snap Peas and Beans with Thai Dressing

1 cup (200 g) dried or 2 cups
  (200 g) drained canned black-
  eyed peas
2 red onions, peeled and sliced
Freshly-squeezed juice of 2
  lemons
1 tablespoon oil
2 teaspoons sesame oil
1 cup (100 g) sugar snap peas or
  snow peas, trimmed
1 green onion (scallion), chopped
1 cup (40 g) mint leaves
1 teaspoon fish sauce
1 teaspoon soy sauce

Serves 4

1 If using dried black-eyed peas, rinse them well and place them in a saucepan. Add enough water to cover and soak overnight. Bring the peas and water to a boil over high heat, then reduce the heat to low and simmer, uncovered, for about 1 hour until tender. Remove from the heat, drain and allow to cool completely. Omit this step if using canned peas.

2 Combine the onion slices and lemon juice in a bowl. Cover and allow to stand for 1 hour.

3 Heat the oils in a wok and stir-fry the sugar snap peas or snow peas over medium heat until tender-crisp, 1–2 minutes. Stir in the black-eyed peas and remove from the heat. Add all the other ingredients and toss until well blended. Transfer to a serving platter and chill in the refrigerator for 30 minutes before serving.

Coconut Puddings with Lime Ginger Syrup

6 ramekins or muffin cups, each
$^1/_2$ cup (125 ml)
Whipped cream (optional), to
serve

Coconut Puddings
$^3/_4$ cup (180 g) butter
$^1/_2$ cup (100 g) superfine (castor)
sugar
1 teaspoon grated lime rind
1 teaspoon vanilla extract (essence)
3 eggs
1 cup (125 g) self-rising flour, sifted
1 cup (75 g) dried unsweetened
grated (desiccated) coconut

Syrup
$^1/_2$ cup (125 g) superfine (castor)
sugar
3 tablespoons freshly-squeezed
lime juice
1 tablespoon finely grated lime
rind
$^1/_3$ in (1 cm) fresh ginger, peeled
and cut into thin shreds

Makes 6

1 Lightly butter the ramekins or muffin cups and line the bottoms with parchment (baking) paper. Set aside.
2 Make the Coconut Puddings by combining the butter, sugar and grated lime rind in a bowl and beating the mixture with an electric mixer until light and creamy, 3–4 minute. Fold in the vanilla extract, then add the eggs, one at a time, and beat well after each addition. If the mixture begins to curdle, add 1 tablespoon of all-purpose flour. Fold in the self-rising flour and grated coconut, and mix well.
3 Spoon the batter into the prepared ramekins or muffin cups and cover each with a piece of buttered parchment paper. Half-fill a wok with water and bring to a rapid boil. Arrange the filled ramekins or muffin cups in a steamer, cover and place the steamer over the boiling water. Steam the Coconut Puddings until firm to the touch, 40–45 minutes, topping up the water in the wok as necessary.
4 To make the Syrup, combine all the ingredients in a small saucepan and heat over low heat, stirring, until the sugar is dissolved. Bring to a boil and allow to simmer uncovered for 2 minutes. Remove from the heat and transfer to a serving jug.
5 Garnish the Coconut Puddings with whipped cream if you like and serve warm with the jug of Syrup on the side. Dribble the Syrup over the Coconut Puddings before eating it.

Zesty Fruit Salad with Spiced Orange Syrup

3 fresh peaches, peeled, pitted
  and sliced
4 fresh figs, quartered
1 cup (200 g) fresh blueberries
2 oranges, peeled and cut into
  segments

Spiced Orange Syrup
1¹/₄ cups (300 ml) water
¹/₂ cup (125 g) superfine (castor)
  sugar
Freshly-squeezed juice and grated
  rind of 1 orange
3 star anise pods
6 whole black peppercorns
6 whole cardamom pods
3 sticks cinnamon

1 Prepare the Spiced Orange Syrup first by combining all the ingredients in a wok and heating the mixture over low heat, stirring, until the sugar is dissolved. Bring the syrup to a boil over medium heat, then reduce the heat and simmer uncovered for 10 minutes. Remove from the heat.

2 Add the fruits to the wok and mix until they are coated well with the syrup. Serve the Fruit Salad warm or chilled.

Serves 4

Polenta Puddings with Mango Sauce

6 ramekins or muffin cups, each
 $1/_2$ cup (125 ml)

Polenta Puddings
$1/_2$ cup (100 g) butter
$3/_4$ cup (150 g) sugar
2 teaspoons grated lemon rind
2 eggs
1 cup (125 g) self-rising flour
$1/_2$ teaspoon baking powder
$1/_4$ teaspoon salt
$2/_3$ cup (100 g) polenta
$1/_2$ cup (125 ml) sour cream
$1/_3$ cup (100 ml) milk

Mango Sauce
2 ripe mangoes, peeled, pitted
 and sliced
2 tablespoons confectioner's
 (icing) sugar
2 tablespoons freshly-squeezed
 lime juice
1 teaspoon grated lime rind

Makes 6

1 Lightly butter the ramekins or muffin cups and line the bottoms with parchment (baking) paper. Set aside.
2 Make the Polenta Puddings by combining the butter, sugar and grated lime rind in a bowl and beating the mixture with an electric mixer until light and creamy, 3–4 minutes. Add the eggs, one at a time, and beat well after each addition. If the mixture begins to curdle, add 1 tablespoon of all-purpose flour.
3 Sift the self-rising flour, baking powder and salt into a bowl and add the polenta. In another bowl, combine the sour cream and milk. Fold the flour mixture into the egg mixture alternately with the sour cream mixture and mix well.
4 Spoon the batter into the prepared ramekins or muffin cups and cover each with a piece of buttered parchment paper. Half-fill a wok with water and bring to a rapid boil. Arrange the filled ramekins or muffin cups in a steamer, cover and place the steamer over the boiling water. Steam the Puddings until firm to the touch, 45–50 minutes, topping up the water in the wok as necessary. Remove the Puddings from the heat and set aside to cool to room temperature.
5 To make the Mango Sauce, process all the ingredients in a food processor until smooth.
6 To serve, run a sharp knife around the sides of each ramekin or muffin cup to loosen, then invert and unmold the Pudding onto a serving platter. Spread the Mango Sauce over the Pudding and serve immediately.

Chinese Doughnuts with Sweet Yogurt Sauce

Sweet Yogurt Sauce

$^3/_4$ cup (200 ml) plain yogurt

1 tablespoon rose water

1 tablespoon confectioner's
(icing) sugar, sifted

Doughnuts

$2^1/_2$ cups (300 g) self-rising flour,
sifted

$^1/_2$ cup (50 g) ground almonds

$^1/_3$ cup (75 g) butter or ghee

$^1/_3$ cup (100 ml) plain yogurt

$^1/_4$ cup (60 ml) warm water

2 teaspoons rose water

Grated rind of 1 orange

Oil or ghee, for deep-frying

$^1/_3$ cup (65 g) superfine (castor)
sugar

Makes 30 doughnuts

1 Prepare the Sweet Yogurt Sauce by combining all the ingredients in a small bowl and mixing well. Cover and refrigerate until ready to serve.

2 To make the Doughnuts, combine the flour and ground almonds in a bowl. Using the fingertips, rub the butter or ghee into the flour and then stir in the yogurt, warm water, rose water and grated orange rind, mixing well to form the mixture into a soft dough. Turn out the dough onto a lightly floured work surface and knead by hands until smooth, about 2 minutes. Roll the dough into cylinders and then divide them into 30 equal pieces. Roll each piece of the dough into a ball.

3 Heat the oil or ghee in a wok to 375 °F (190 °C)—the oil is ready when a bread cube dropped in it sizzles on contact. Deep-fry the Doughnuts, a few at a time, until golden, 5–6 minutes. Remove from the hot oil and drain on paper towels.

4 Place the sugar in a plate and roll each deep-fried Doughnut in the sugar until well coated. Serve warm with the Yogurt Sauce.

Complete List of Recipes